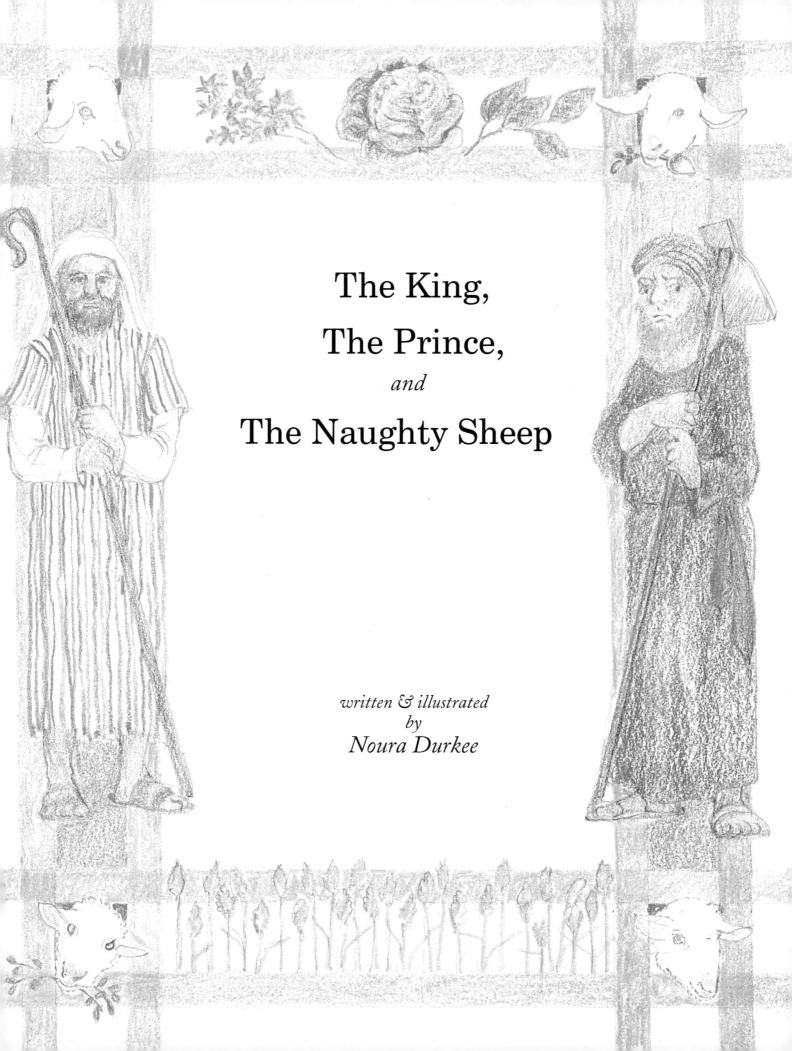

The King,
The Prince,
and
The Naughty Sheep

written & illustrated
by
Noura Durkee

The King,
the Prince
and
the Naughty Sheep

Published by

Tahrike Tarsile Quran Inc.
Publishers and Distributors of The Qur'an
P.O. Box 73115
Elmhurst, New York 11373-0115

author & illustrator: Noura Durkee

First U.S. Edition 1999
Library of Congress Catalog Number: 98-061664
British Library Cataloguing in Publication Data
ISBN: 1-879402-58-0

References to Dawood and Sulayman ﷺ in the Qur'an:
This story is mentioned in Surah 21:78-79. Its details are filled in
by many stories from the Companions of the Prophet Muhammad ﷺ,
who all agreed about its meaning; it has been passed on to us by
the commentaries of the scholars of Qur'an.
There are many other references to Dawood and Sulayman ﷺ in the
Qur'an. Dawood: 6:84, 21:80, 34:10-11, 38:17-26, 2:251.
Sulayman: 2:102, 6:84, 21:81-82, 27:15-44, 34:12-14, 38:30-40.

Muslims say certain phrases to ask the blessings of Allah
on the prophets and a few other righteous people. They
are said whenever the name of the person is mentioned.
Those used in this story are:

ﷺ: 'alayhi-s-salam: peace be upon him
ﷺ: 'alayhuma-s-salam: peace be upon them both

Dawood was king in Jerusalem, and he had a son named Sulayman ﷺ. Both of them were prophets, helping their people with messages from Allah.

Allah loved Dawood ﷺ so much that He told the birds and the mountains to sing with him.

Allah loved Sulayman ﷺ so much that He gave him all sorts of surprising powers. He let him order the jinn to build wonderful buildings.

But best of all, Allah taught Sulayman  the languages of birds and animals.

He used to love to listen to their conversations.

"While he does that, the farmer can
take care of the sheep and have their milk
and lambs and wool. That will pay the farmer
for his lost plants."

"When all the vegetables and grains are growing again, they can trade back.
The farmer will be a farmer again, and the shepherd will have his sheep. That's all!"

The farmer smiled a big smile.
He thought that was fair.
The shepherd smiled too. After a little while, he would have his sheep back.
The king smiled. Sulayman ﷺ smiled.

Prince Sulayman  and his father King Dawood 🙵 got along very well. Even when Sulayman 🙵 was only a young boy, the king used to let him come along when he travelled. He used to let his son sit with him when he was listening to the people.

People came with all sorts of troubles.
They came when they needed money.
They came when they lost something.
They came when they were having arguments.
They wanted the king to fix EVERYTHING.

King Dawood ﷺ listened patiently to all
their problems. He was very fair.
He tried to help each person.
Sulayman ﷺ listened too.
He watched carefully.
He wanted to learn.

One day, when Sulayman ﷺ was eleven years old, a farmer and a shepherd and a lot of sheep came to see the king. Sulayman ﷺ liked the sheep. They had curly wool coats and long tails and kept saying BAAA-A-A-AAA!

BAAA-A-A-AAA!

BAAA-A-A-AAA!

The farmer spoke first. He was VERY angry.
His face was all red and he talked
in a loud voice.

He said,

"This shepherd wasn't watching his sheep!
They came into my beautiful garden!
They ate my lettuce
and my parsley
and my carrots
and sat in the wheat
and nibbled the grain!
My garden is ruined
and I will have nothing to sell
and nothing to eat!"

The king turned to the shepherd.
The shepherd was angry too,
but he was angry at the sheep.

"These dumb animals went
through a hole
in the fence!

They got into his garden in
the middle of the night!"

"It's not my fault,
if I have to sleep a little!"

The sheep kept quiet.

They didn't even say BA-A-A-a-a after that.
But they weren't ashamed.

They were remembering the lovely garden
and what a very good time they had
eating it all up!

Ahhh, they thought to themselves.
The red radishes.

The sweet grass.

The beautiful lettuce.

The tender peas.

And the parsley!!

The king thought for a minute and then said,

"The garden is spoiled, so the farmer has no crop.
The shepherd's sheep ruined the garden.
The shepherd must give his sheep to the farmer."

"My life is finished!" wailed the shepherd.
"What good is a shepherd without sheep?"
And he began to cry.

Sulayman  was sitting beside his father.
He tugged his sleeve.
King Dawood ﷺ leaned down and listened
while his son whispered something in his ear.
The king nodded.

Sulayman ﷺ whispered again,
and the king nodded again, and smiled.
Then the king spoke.

"We have a better idea.
The plants are spoiled, but the garden is still there.
New plants can grow in it.
The farmer still has something.
But the shepherd can't grow new sheep,
if he has to give them all away!
He won't have anything, and that isn't fair.
So, we will do it this way:
the shepherd will take care of the garden.
He will clean it all up and plant new seeds.
He will work very hard, just as if
it all belonged to him."

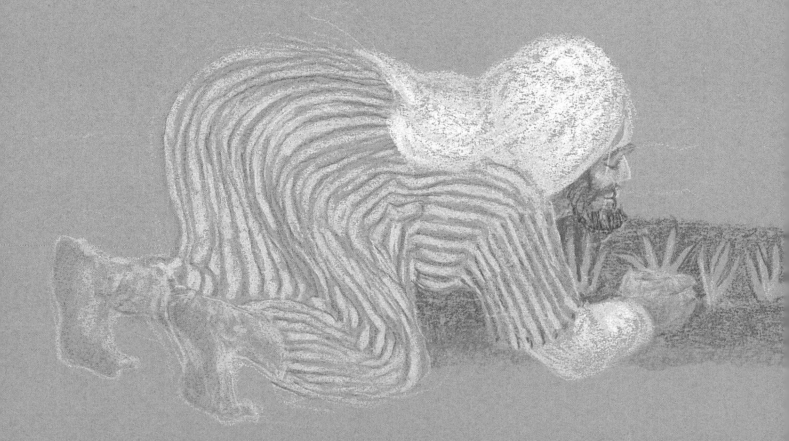

The sheep looked at one another and said,

BAAA-A-A-AA!"

and everybody went home.